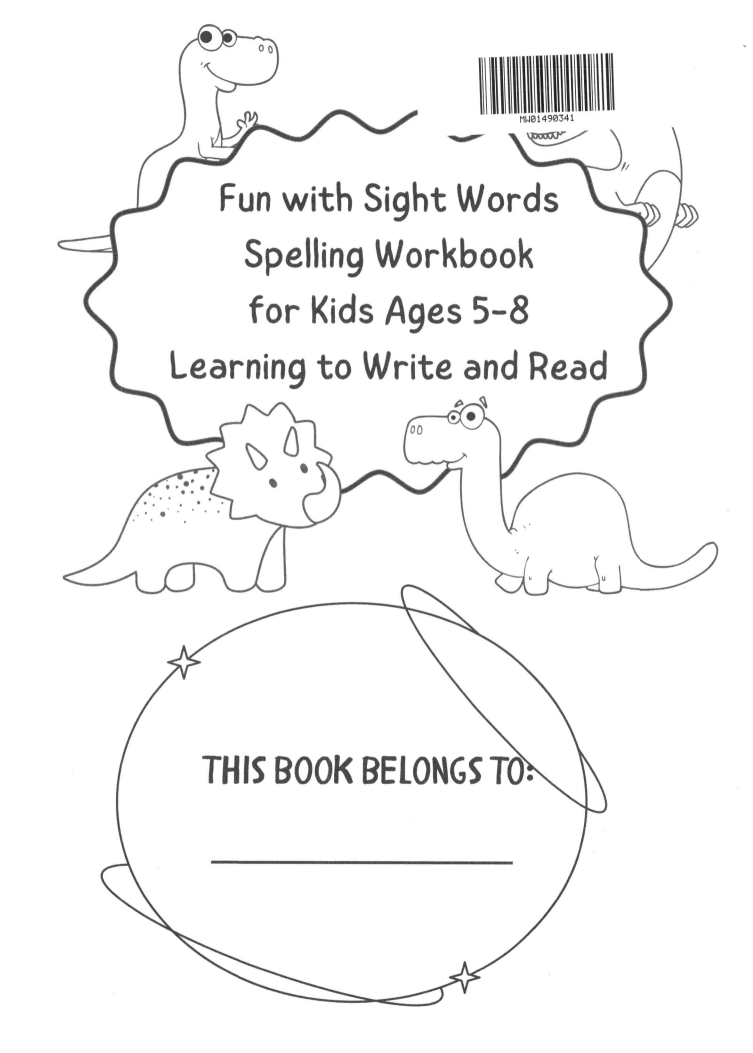

Fun with Sight Words
Spelling Workbook
for Kids Ages 5-8
Learning to Write and Read

THIS BOOK BELONGS TO:

_____

Contents

Introduction

Thank you for buying this book.

You have just found a fun and easy way to teach your child how to read and write the most common, high frequency words and practice sentences with them.

With the help of this book, he or she is guided step by step through the whole process of learning, from tracing dotted lines to writing all by themselves.

The whole practice is progressive, starting from one letter words, up to even nine letter word.

It is divided into two parts:

1. Containing words from 1 to 100 and suitable for ages 5-7
2. Containing words from 101 to 200 and suitable for ages 7-8

Let the child work at their own pace, read aloud, and go through 3 steps:

1. Trace and write on their own the letters of the alphabet
2. Trace and write on their own the words
3. Trace and write on their own the sentences with the sight words

The book contains, in addition, nice pictures to color, word scramble activities, and pages to creatively draw your own images.

Adult guidance is needed but Smiley – the little dinosaur will encourage your child as well along the way.

You can download bonus activity pages after clicking on the QR code at the end of the book.

Included is also a certificate of completion that could be an additional reward for the brave little learner and will make them proud of their accomplishment.

Hi! I'm Smiley. We'll be learning to read and write together. Join me!

ABCDEFGHIJ **KLMNOPQRSTUVWXYZ**

ABCDEFGHIJKLMNOPQRSTUVWXYZ

a b c d e f g h i j **k l m n o p q r s t u v w x y z**

a b c d e f g h i j k l m n o p q r s t u v w x y z

a I have a cat.

a a a a a a a a a a a a a

a a a a a a a a a a a a a

I have a cat.

I have a cat. I have a cat

I have a cat. I have a cat

I I like animals.

I I I I I I I I I I I I I

I I I I I I I I I I I I I

I like animals.

I like animals.

am

I am happy.

am am am am am am am

I am happy.

an

This is an apple.

an an an an an an an an

This is an apple.

as   I am as strong as an ox.

as as as as as as as

I am as strong as an ox.

at   Look at the cake!

at at at at at at at at

Look at the cake!

be

I want to be an astronaut.

be be be be be be be

I want to be an astronaut.

by

Sit by the tree.

by by by by by by by by

Sit by the tree.

do
What would you like to do?

do do do do do do do

What would you like to do?

go
I go swimming every day.

go go go go go go go go go

I go swimming every day.

he

He is very nice.

he he he he he he he

He is very nice.

if

If you like cookies, try these.

if if if if if if if if

If you like cookies, try these.

in   The present is in the box.

in in in in in in in

The present is in the box.

is   Is it sunny?

is is is is is is is is

Is it sunny?

it   It is a nice car.

it it it it it it it

It is a nice car.

my   Do you like my picture?

my my my my my my my

Do you like my picture?

no

I can see no kids.

no no no no no no no

I can see no kids.

of

This is a game of cards.

of of of of of of of of of

This is a game of cards.

on The book is on the table.

on on on on on on on on

The book is on the table.

or Would you like a pen or a toy?

or or or or or or or

Would you like a pen or a toy?

so I am so lucky!

so so so so so so so

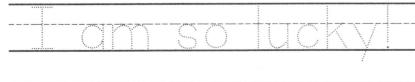 I am so lucky!

to I like going to school.

to to to to to to to

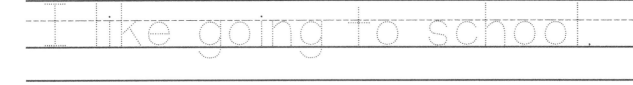 I like going to school.

up

The bird is up in the sky.

up up up up up up up

The bird is up in the sky.

we

We like each other.

we we we we we we we

We like each other.

all

I like all my toys.

all all all all all all all

I like all my toys.

and

I have pens and pencils.

and and and and and and

I have pens and pencils.

are   Are you smiling?

are are are are are are

Are you smiling?

but   I like water, but prefer juice.

but but but but but but

I like water, but prefer juice.

can

Can we go camping?

can can can can can can

Can we go camping?

day

We have fun every day.

day day day day day day

We have fun every day.

did

Did you go to school yesterday?

did did did did did did

Did you go to school yesterday?

for

This book is for you.

for for for for for for

This book is for you.

get

Would you like to get a new bike?

get get get get get get

Would you like to get a new bike?

had

We had a good time.

had had had had had had

We had a good time.

has

My friend has a nice dog.

has has has has has has

My friend has a nice dog.

her

Is it her ball?

her her her her her her

Is it her ball?

him

Will you play with him?

him him him him him him

Will you play with him?

his

This is his schoolbag.

his his his his his his

This is his schoolbag.

how

How do you like this workbook?

how how how how how

How do you like this workbook?

its

This is its food.

its its its its its its

This is its food.

may

May you help me?

may may may may may

May you help me?

not

This is not an elephant.

not not not not not not

This is not an elephant.

now   I would like to go home now.

now now now now now

I would like to go home now

one   I have one sister.

one one one one one one

I have one sister.

out Would you like to go out?

out out out out out

Would you like to go out?

see I can see a bee.

see see see see see

I can see a bee.

she

She loves school.

she she she she she

She loves school.

the

Look at the farm!

the the the the the

Look at the farm!

two

I have two hamsters.

two two two two two

I have two hamsters.

use

Do you use this computer?

use use use use use

Do you use this computer?

was

I was at home.

was was was was was

I was at home.

way

Is this the way to your house?

way way way way way

Is this the way to your house?

you

Do you play basketball?

you you you you you

Do you play basketball?

been

Have you been to a ball?

been been been been been

Have you been to a ball?

come

Come with us!

come come come come

Come with us!

down

I will go down this hill.

down down down down

I will go down this hill.

each

Do you like each other?

each each each each

Do you like each other?

find

He wants to find his pencil.

find find find find

He wants to find his pencil.

from

Where are you from?

from from from from

Where are you from?

have

Have fun at school!

have have have have

Have fun at school!

44

Bravo!
Now draw a picture with your favourite sentence.

into

She is putting her toys into a box.

into into into into

She is putting her toys into a box.

like

Me and my friends like playing.

like like like like

Me and my friends like playing.

long

It is a long snake.

long long long long

It is a long snake.

look

Look at my teacher!

look look look look

Look at my teacher!

made

It is made of wood.

made made made made

It is made of wood.

make

Can we make a cake?

make make make make

Can we make a cake?

many How many cows can you see?

many many many many

How many cows can you see?

more Have you got more ice cream?

more more more more

Have you got more ice cream?

part

Which part of the tree is it?

part part part part

Which part of the tree is it?

said

The parrot said hello.

said said said said

The parrot said hello.

some   Have you got some cheese?

some some some some

Have you got some cheese?

than   I am faster than the tortoise.

than than than than

I am faster than the tortoise.

that

Look at that!

that that that that

Look at that!

them

I like them.

them them them them

I like them.

then

I will have lunch and then go outside.

then then then then

I will have lunch and then go outside.

they

They like computers.

they they they they

They like computers.

this

Is this your doll?

this this this this

Is this your doll?

time

What time is it?

time time time time

What time is it?

were   Were you at home in the morning?

were were were were

Were you at home in the morning?

what   What did you learn?

what what what what

What did you learn?

Fantastic!

Now write a sentence of your own with the word make and draw it.

when

When do you eat your dinner?

when when when when

When do you eat your dinner?

with

I love playing with my dog.

with with with with

I love playing with my dog.

will   Will you come to the party?

will will will will

Will you come to the party?

your   Is this your mum?

your your your your

Is this your mum?

58

about

What are you talking about?

about about about about

What are you talking about?

first

My sister is in the first grade. ①

first first first first

My sister is in the first grade.

could

I could sing a song.

could could could could

I could sing a song.

other

I want the other book

other other other other

I want the other book.

their

They love their fish.

their their their their

They love their fish.

there

Look over there!

there there there there

Look over there!

these

These sentences are easy.

these these these these

These sentences are easy.

water

Do you drink water?

water water water water

Do you drink water?

which — Which animal do you like the best?

which which which which

Which animal do you like best?

words — I love learning words.

words words words words

I love learning words.

would

Would you like to have lunch?

would would would would

Would you like to have lunch?

write

I can write well.

write write write write

I can write well.

called

He called his dad.

called called called called

He called his dad.

number

Which number is it?

number number number

Which number is it?

people
How many people can you see?

people people people

How many people can you see?

almost
It is almost night.

almost almost almost

It is almost night.

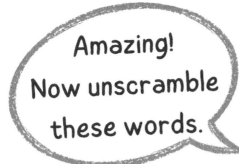

Amazing! Now unscramble these words.

THEM WOULD CALLED WORDS MADE FIRST THESE YOUR THIS THERE TIME SOME ABOUT MANY WILL

1. AELLDC...
2. BOTUA...
3. TEHER...
4. EMIT...
5. LODWU...
6. WROSD...
7. ETSHE...
8. YORU...
9. LLWI...
10. IHST...
11. THEM...
12. IFTSR...
13. MEOS...
14. NMAY...
15. AEDM...

me   Give me the pen, please.

me me me me me me me

Give me the pen, please.

us   Will you show us your room?

us us us us us us us us

Will you show us your room?

air   Look at that hot air balloon!

air air air air air air air

Look at that hot air balloon!

any   Have you got any brothers?

any any any any any any

Have you got any brothers?

69

ask

Ask him about his school.

ask ask ask ask ask ask

Ask him about his school.

big

This hippo is really big!

big big big big big big

This hippo is really big!

boy   Are you a good boy?

boy boy boy boy boy boy

Are you a good boy?

end   This is the end of the story.

end end end end end end

This is the end of the story.

man

Do you know this man?

man man man man man

Do you know this man?

men

My uncles are nice men.

men men men men men

My uncles are nice men.

new   I have a new toy.

new new new new new

I have a new toy.

off   Get off the bus now.

off off off off off off off

Get off the bus now.

old

This is an old shoe.

old old old old old old old old

This is an old shoe.

our

Our family is the best!

our our our our our our

Our family is the best!

put

Put your things away.

put put put put put put

Put your things away.

say

Say goodbye to your friends.

say say say say say say

Say goodbye to your friends.

set

I can set the table.

set set set set set set

I can set the table.

too

This shirt is too long.

too too too too too too

This shirt is too long.

try   Try writing this on your own.

try try try try try try

Try writing this on your own.

why   Why do you learn to read?

why why why why why

Why do you learn to read?

also

Do you also like writing?

also also also also also

Do you also like writing?

away

Tell this dragon to go away.

away away away away

Tell this dragon to go away.

back

We are back to school.

back back back back

We are back to school.

came

We came here to play tennis.

came came came came

We came here to play tennis.

does   Does she like running?

does does does does

Does she like running?

even   I like school, even homework.

even even even even

I like school, even homework.

form

Can you form the letter A?

form form form form

Can you form the letter A?

give

Can you give me your pencil?

give give give give give

Can you give me your pencil?

good

Are you a good student?

good good good good

Are you a good student?

hand

Can you see my hand?

hand hand hand hand

Can you see my hand?

help

Can you help your mother?

help help help help help

Can you help your mother?

here

I would like to sit here.

here here here here here

I would like to sit here.

home

I like learning at home.

home home home home

I like learning at home.

just

We have just finished dinner.

just just just just just

We have just finished dinner.

kind   What kind of books do you like?

kind kind kind kind kind

What kind of books do you like?

land   The plane will land soon.

land land land land land

The plane will land soon.

learn

I would like to learn to cook.

learn learn learn learn

I would like to learn to cook.

line

I can write on this line. Aa

line line line line line line

I can write on this line.

live

Where does a monkey live?

live live live live live live

Where does a monkey live?

most

I like most food.

most most most most

I like most food.

move   Can you move your ears?

move move move move

Can you move your ears?

much   Do you read much?

much much much much

Do you read much?

must   I must finish this book today.

must must must must

I must finish this book today.

name   Do you know his name?

name name name name

Do you know his name?

need   They need a new car.

need need need need

They need a new car.

only   I have only one computer.

only only only only only

I have only one computer.

over

The birds are over the tree.

over over over over

The birds are over the tree.

page

Which page is it?

page page page page

Which page is it?

play

Would you like to play the piano?

play play play play play

Would you like to play the piano?

read

Will you read it for me?

read read read read

Will you read it for me?

same
These horses are the same.

same same same same

These horses are the same.

show
Will you show me your picture?

show show show show

Will you show me your picture?

such

I love such books!

such such such such

I love such books!

take

Can you take this with you?

take take take take

Can you take this with you?

tell

I can tell the time.

tell tell tell tell tell

I can tell the time.

turn

You must turn right.

turn turn turn turn

You must turn right.

very   This word is very easy.

very very very very

This word is very easy.

want   Do you want to be a doctor?

want want want want

Do you want to be a doctor?

well

I can write well.

well well well well well

I can write well.

went

They went shopping.

went went went went

They went shopping.

Good job!

Now draw a picture with your favourite sentence.

work   My mum has to work.

work work work work

My mum has to work.

know   I know how to ride a bike.

know know know know

I know how to ride a bike.

after
Number one is after number two.

12

after after after after

Number one is after number two.

again
I have to come back here again.

again again again again

I have to come back here again.

found

He found his keys.

found found found found

He found his keys.

great

I have great sisters.

great great great great

I have great sisters.

house

My house is very pretty.

house house house

My house is very pretty.

large

I have a large schoolbag.

large large large large

I have a large schoolbag.

means I want to know what he means.

means means means

I want to know what he means.

place   This is the place I want to go.

place place place place

This is the place I want to go.

point   Point to the letter C.   **C G K**

point point point point

Point to the letter C.

right   Do I have to turn right or left?

right right right right

Do I have to turn right or left?

small

Do you like small children?

small small small small

Do you like small children?

sound

Listen to this sound.

sound sound sound sound

Listen to this sound.

spell Can he spell the word story? **STORY**

spell spell spell spell spell

Can he spell the word story?

still Does your friend still play baseball?

still still still still still

Does your friend still play baseball?

study

Do you study maths?

`1+2=3`

study study study study

Do you study maths?

think

I think this bike looks nice.

think think think think

I think this bike looks nice.

three

I have three good friends.

three three three three

I have three good friends.

where

Where is your home?

where where where where

Where is your home?

High five!

Now write a sentence of your own with the word help and draw it.

world — Would you like to see the world?

world world world world

Would you like to see the world?

years — Is your mum 30 years old? 30

years years years years

Is your mum 30 years old?

animal

Is a frog a nice animal?

animal animal animal animal

Is a frog a nice animal?

answer

Answer yes or no.

YES NO

answer answer answer

Answer yes or no.

around The dog is following the cat around.

around around around

The dog is following the cat around.

before The letter A is before B. ABC

before before before

The letter A is before B.

change Can you write the word change? **CHANGE**

change change change

Can you write the word change?

follow Will you follow me? **FOLLOW**

follow follow follow follow

Will you follow me?

letter I like writing the letter W the most. W

letter letter letter letter

I like writing the letter W the most.

little Are you still little?

little little little little

Are you still little?

mother My mother is the best in the world!

mother mother mother

My mother is the best in the world!

should   Should you help you dad?   WORLD'S BEST DAD

should should should

Should you help your dad?

things

Do you need many things?

things things things

Do you need many things?

America

Does he live in America?

America America America

Does he live in America?

another Would you like another banana?

another another another

Would you like another banana?

because I like books because they are fun.

because because because

I like books because they are fun.

picture   Draw a picture.

picture picture picture

Draw a picture.

through   They went through the park.

through through through

They went through the park.

sentence This is the sentence I like the most. ♡

sentence sentence

This is the sentence I like the most.

different I prefer a different time.

different different

I prefer a different time.

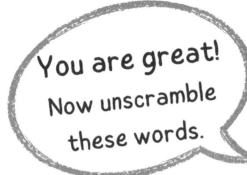

You are great! Now unscramble these words.

HOUSE SENTENCE CAME YEARS FOUND LARGE THREE SMALL AWAY THINK WORLD WHERE STILL EVEN STUDY

1. AAWY..

2. ACEM...

3. VENE...

4. EOSHU..

5. ODUFN...

6. LERAG..

7. WEHER...

8. AMLLS...

9. TEERH..

10. ROWLD..

11. CTEESENN......................................

12. SAYRE...

13. SILLT...

14. SYTUD...

15. TNIKH...

Sight words 1-100 age 5-7

a	13	and	26	was	40	they	53
I	13	are	27	way	40	this	54
am	14	but	27	you	41	time	54
an	14	can	28	been	41	were	55
as	15	day	28	come	42	what	55
at	15	did	29	down	42	when	57
be	16	for	29	each	43	with	57
by	16	get	30	find	43	will	58
do	17	had	30	from	44	your	58
go	17	has	31	have	44	about	59
he	18	her	31	into	46	first	59
if	18	him	32	like	46	could	60
in	19	his	32	long	47	other	60
is	19	how	33	look	47	their	61
it	20	its	33	made	48	there	61
my	20	may	35	make	48	these	62
no	21	not	35	many	49	water	62
of	21	now	36	more	49	which	63
on	22	one	36	part	50	words	63
or	22	out	37	said	50	would	64
so	24	see	37	some	51	write	64
to	24	she	38	than	51	called	65
up	25	the	38	that	52	number	65
we	25	two	39	them	52	people	66
all	26	use	39	then	53	almost	66

Sight words 101-200 age 7-8

me	68	even	81	same	95	still	108
us	68	form	82	show	95	study	109
air	69	give	82	such	96	think	109
any	69	good	83	take	96	three	110
ask	70	hand	83	tell	97	where	110
big	70	help	84	turn	97	world	112
boy	71	here	84	very	98	years	112
end	71	home	85	want	98	animal	113
man	72	just	85	well	99	answer	113
men	72	kind	86	went	99	around	114
new	73	land	86	work	101	before	114
off	73	learn	87	know	101	change	115
old	74	line	87	after	102	follow	115
our	74	live	88	again	102	letter	116
put	75	most	88	found	103	little	116
say	75	move	90	great	103	mother	117
set	76	much	90	house	104	should	117
too	76	must	91	large	104	things	118
try	77	name	91	means	105	America	118
why	77	need	92	place	105	another	119
also	79	only	92	point	106	because	119
away	79	over	93	right	106	picture	120
back	80	page	93	small	107	through	120
came	80	play	94	sound	107	sentence	121
does	81	read	94	spell	108	different	121

Thank you again for choosing this book.

If you would like to get free activity pages, please email me at:

bonniemaygoodman@gmail.com

or scan the QR code

Congratulations!
Let's celebrate now!

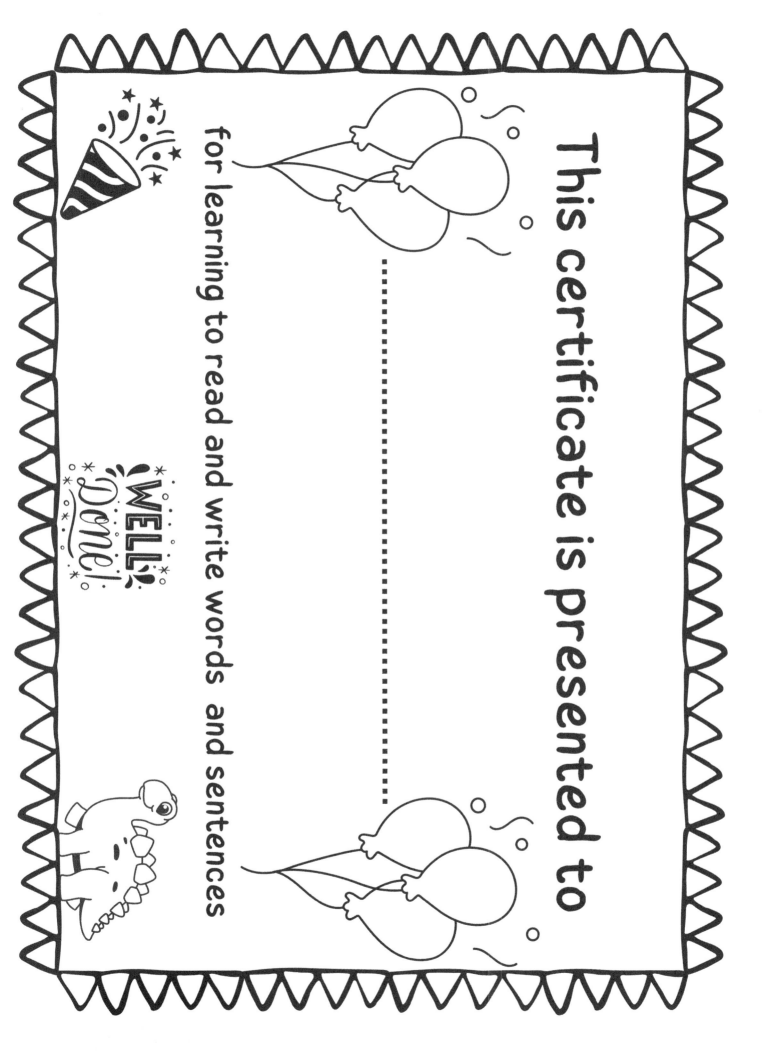

This certificate is presented to

for learning to read and write words and sentences

WELL Done!

Made in United States
North Haven, CT
16 October 2022

25456145R00070